THE
PING PONG GAME

THE
PING PONG GAME

Solutions "A Better Way"

By: JAMES SAMMARTINO

authorHOUSE®

AuthorHouse™
1663 Liberty Drive
Bloomington, IN 47403
www.authorhouse.com
Phone: 1-800-839-8640

Published by AuthorHouse   10/18/2012

ISBN: 978-1-4772-8104-8 (sc)
ISBN: 978-1-4772-8105-5 (e)

Library of Congress Control Number: 2012919469

CONTENTS

Introduction vii

A Need For Change 1
The Ping Pong Game 5
Is The Glass Half Empty Or Half Full? 10
Optinomics Versus Pessinomics! 12
The Cure Is The Cause! 16
Discovering The Lemons! 19
What Is Money? 23
Inflation 30
The First Lemon . . . Taxes 35
The Proper Recipe! 41
Democracy The Logical Choice! 46
A Matter Of Common Sense! 60
The 2nd Lemon-The Federal Reserve! 65
Would You If You Could? 69
The New World Order 74
The American Wealth Card! 80
We The People! 90
The Cva And The Votery 94
Changing The World One Vote At A Time 98
To Dream The Impossible Dream 100
What's It Really All About? 105
When Is Enough . . . Enough 108
The Members Pledge 111
The Representatives Pledge 113
The Beginning 115

INTRODUCTION

Welcome to The American Evolution, a new eco-political philosophy for the 21st century.

The American Evolution is about our future and whether "We The People" will continue to allow our Constitution to be dismantled, or whether we can join together and put a stop to it.

The American Evolution is about logic, reason, and common sense and whether "We The People" can use these God given gifts, or whether we remain content with what not using them creates

The American Evolution is about the examination of failure proven economics that only work for some of the people some of the time and whether "We The People" will create new economic policies that will work for all of the people, all of the time.

The American Evolution is about continuing to elect leaders that divide us into states of red and blue, or whether "We The People" will elect leaders that unite us into states of Red, White and Blue.

The American Evolution is about choice and what "We The People" will choose.

If America is ever to be all that it can be, we the American people must make a choice. Whether you are a Democrat, Republican, Capitalist, Socialist, Conservative, Liberal, Libertarian, or whatever does not really matter. What does matter is what we choose for our future. Do we continue to choose the results and havoc of economics and politics that do not use logic, reason and common sense, or do we opt for change and the use of political and economic formulas that do?

We hold these truths to be self evident—that all men are created equal, that they are endowed by their Creator with certain unalienable Rights, that among these are Life, Liberty and the pursuit of Happiness—That to secure these rights, Governments are instituted among Men, deriving their just powers from the consent of the governed.

In this one paragraph is a summation of what it means to be an American. What do you think Americans desire? Do they desire a Government that is to be of the people, by the people, and for the people . . . deriving their just powers from the consent of the governed to secure the Rights of Life, Liberty and the Pursuit of Happiness, or do they desire a government that is allowed to do whatever it desires?

Unfortunately for too long we have been split on how to secure these Rights of Life, Liberty and the Pursuit of Happiness. On one hand, we are a nation of people with compassion and a sincere desire to offer hope and help to the less fortunate. On the other hand, we are a nation of people that resents being told what to do with our money and the fruits of our labor. The real question is this . . . Must we choose between the two? The simple answer to this question is . . . NO . . . we do not.

A NEED FOR CHANGE

There is no doubt that there is a need for change. I am not talking about a change in economic policy from one political party to the other, but one of real economic and political change! Economic and political changes that will create new policies that are based on logic, reason and common sense. Economic and political policies for us to use that not only take advantage of our natural and human resources, but changes that also take advantage of our technology too. New economic policies that will produce real solutions to most, and possibly all of the major problems facing us today! Changes from a politics of political parties that divide us, to a new politics that will unite us. After all, are we the Divided States of America, or the United States of America?

Changes with solutions that include:

An end to our hunger problem

An end the problems of the homeless

Diminishing and even eliminating poverty altogether

Reduced crime

Eliminating foreclosure

Providing research money for cancer and all diseases

Eliminating taxes on the rich, poor and middle class

No more national debt

Putting and end to our illegal alien problems

Controlling inflation

Providing social security to the sick and the elderly

Job assurance for all Americans

Providing whatever is needed for our self-defense

Providing FREE and universal healthcare for all Americans

Providing FREE and universal education for all Americans

Insuring freedoms guaranteed in the Constitution

Recreating a government of, by and for the people

Creating an even higher standard of living for all Americans

How wonderful would achieving these things be, and why aren't our present political candidates addressing them?

It must also be understood that we can never achieve any significant or real change until we first understand and change how wealth is created and distributed in America today. What also must be made perfectly clear is that we can never allow ALL THE PEOPLE to achieve anything until we change economics and politics that prevent it by limiting it. Whenever we limit, someone or something is left out. This is what limiting means. This simple but true statement LIMITING LEAVES OUT is the cause of all our problems in a nutshell!

It should also now be clear that unless we change from a Representative Republic to a Democratic Republic, or better still to a Protectorate form of government, we can never be a government of the people, by the people and for the people.

For those who doubt the wisdom of this, all you need to do to dispel those doubts is to use your logic, reason and common sense. The answer can be found by asking two simple questions. The first one is, do you want to be ruled by a government, or do you want to have your rights and freedoms protected? The second question is, who is the best person to vote on the laws that affect you? Is it some dictator or king, a small group of people, or you? My logic, reason, and common sense demand that I fight not only for real economic changes, it also demands that I must fight for real political changes too. What does your logic, reason, and common sense demand?

Does it demand things remain insane? By definition insanity is to continue to do things the same way as in the past, and expect the results to be different. Perhaps you are content with being apathetic and will continue to do nothing, but is that not just as insane? Perhaps you have faith in our present system and reject logic, reason and common sense. However, if you truly wish to stop the insanity then you must join us in achieving what some believe is an impossible dream. That dream is for us to give up the labels that divide us and unite together to make the changes we need, want, and know we can achieve.

THE PING PONG GAME

Since the founding of America, two major political philosophies continue to ping pong power back and forth without any major problems being solved. We still struggle with escalating crime, unemployment, high taxes, poverty, the homeless, hunger, and the devastation of war. We even have some problems our founding fathers did not have, such as an economic debt in the trillions of dollars.

Is it possible for us to use our God given gifts of logic, reason and common sense to create a new set of economic laws to follow, or are we somehow mysteriously bound to using outdated methods and economic policies that defy logic, reason, and common sense?

Should we blindly continue to follow an economic formula developed in the 18th century? A century without the benefit of the radio, TV, computer, phone, Internet and all the other technological marvels of today! I don't think so. I think we should objectively analyze the effects of those economic policies as they impact us today. If you agree then just what is it that stops us from coming together and bringing our economic policy in line with our technological advances?

It is my belief that the majority of the American people hold that as good as we have it here in this country, things can and should be much better. What do you believe? Is there room for improvement? If you agree that there is room for improvement, the next question is this . . . How do we make these improvements? For some reason we have been unable to create real significant change. We still have poverty, crime, burdensome taxes, increasing inflation, a national debt, unemployment and go to war. With the exception of technological advances, which have made everyone's life better, there haven't been any significant changes in our economic laws and politics in over 200 years.

It also hasn't mattered who's in charge. We have had the Liberals, Republicans, Democrats, and Conservatives in charge, and neither the party nor the philosophy seems to matter. The rich are still getting richer, the poor are still increasing in numbers, and the middle class is still bearing the tax burden. Could that be because no matter who is in charge, they all follow the same laws of economics that have not worked in the past over and over, and over again? Economic policies that are designed at best to only provide a temporary shift in benefits from one segment of the country to the other, but never lasting significant benefits to all. Since this is true, and undeniably so, how does it make any sense to continue to do things the same way in the future, if they have not worked in the past, regardless of what political party or philosophy is in charge?

To expect the future to change for the better without changing what has not worked in the past is not only insane, it is very foolish too, and yet, we keep doing it over, and over, and over again! Why? Why do we continue to do this? Will there ever come a time when we the American people wake up, have that light bulb go on over our heads, slap ourselves on the forehead and just go duh!

Given the technology that we have today and that which is right around the corner, we cannot only provide for the necessities of life, we can provide for most, and perhaps even all of our material desires as well. The only thing stopping us from changing for the better is our own self-imposed limitation. Changing for the better is as simple as doing it. Once this is realized, the next step is a rather simple one. That step is for us to simply prioritize and determine what we should change, why we should change it, and how we should do it.

Since logic dictates that if we are ever to allow all the people to prosper and not only allow some to prosper by causing others to go without, what needs to be absolutely clear is that one of the very first things we must do, is eliminate limited money supply economics.

Since money is what we use to produce, sell, and buy all of our goods and services, when we limit the production of money, we allow only some of the people to have access to all the money they may need or want by making it impossible for others to do so.

When talking about monetary change, it is not only imperative that we create a money supply that is sufficient to allow all the people the ability to obtain their needs and wants, it is just as important to insure that all those people who need money will have access to it too.

This fact is very important, and just can't be repeated enough. It must also be really understood if anything else that follows is to make sense. It is our adherence to limited money supply economics that is the reason why we have the financial problems that we do. To understand this let's look at the problem of hunger in America today. In America there is an abundance of food, right?

It is also unfortunate but very true that Americans are actually dying from malnutrition and American children are going to bed hungry. Why is this so? Do you believe it is because of our inability to produce food? Is it with our inability to create money, which can be done digitally in an instant? Absolutely not! The problem is caused by the results of the limited money supply economics by which the food must be obtained. Any economic policy that intentionally limits the obtaining of food, as people go hungry and literally starve to death, in a just society should be considered a crime against humanity.

Using limited money supply economics we create a fixed wealth by fixing the amount of money in circulation. This is done to stimulate competition and curb inflation. While stimulating competition has been a very effective way of producing goods and services, and curbing inflation is admirable, doing so by limiting the distribution of money has proven to be a very costly one . . . too costly. This is because of the results it achieves. Results like hunger amidst an abundance of food.

IS THE GLASS HALF EMPTY OR HALF FULL?

If America is ever to be all that it can be, we the people must make a choice of perception . . . . Is our glass half empty or half full?

Using today's computer technology, it is no longer necessary to ping pong back and forth a fixed wealth and fixed money supply to motivate productivity or to curb inflation. In order to achieve the real economic prosperity we desire, as a nation we must pursue a new course. We must find a way that does not limit. A way that does not leave someone out, prevent the rich from getting richer, nor anyone from obtaining the necessities of life or achieving the American Dream.

Excepting for the great depression, never before in the history of our nation have things been so good and so bad for so many. America today secures its freedom through a military strength unlike anything ever seen. It is a country capable of discovering the cure for polio, splitting the atom, and conquering the depths of space. Today's American enjoys the most luxurious conveniences that technology has to offer. These conveniences include heat to keep us warm, AC to keep us cool, large screen TV's, wireless phones, personal computers, exquisite cars, world travel and more. Just about anything that is desired is available for the taking. That is of course . . . if you have the money.

But there is also this other America. A country losing its people to war and disease, a nation with hunger and homeless, a nation riddled with crime and poverty. The same country that houses the most self-made millionaires is also the home for the most who abuse drugs. How is it possible that the same nation can inspire some people to achieve so much, and others to achieve so little? For those in this country who "have", the answer is simple. The "have-nots" are lazy, addicted, or dysfunctional. The reason for their poverty is of their own choosing. Those who are "have-nots" may claim bad luck, discrimination or a host of other reasons behind their failure.

Although founded on offering hope and not despair, we are a nation that is fast becoming increasingly more pessimistic. Whether you are blue or red, liberal or conservative, or something in between, doesn't really matter. What does matter is what we choose. Do we continue to bear the results and havoc of failure proven economic laws and formulas that do not use logic, reason and common sense, or do we sweep the floor clean and create new laws of economics and formulas based upon principles that do?

OPTINOMICS VERSUS PESSINOMICS!

Generally speaking, people fall into two categories. They are either optimistic or pessimistic. The economic pessimists or Pessinomics are lost in the past. They hold on to old school thinking, believing war is good for the economy, that money needs to be backed by gold and silver and that our demand is greater than our ability to supply it. If war is so good for the economy why not have New York declare war on California? With 50 states we can create 25 wars.

I call the new economics of The American Evolution . . . "Optinomics". I also call myself an Optinomic because I believe there is a solution to any problem; we just need to find it. I also believe that working together to find that solution is better than working against each other, fighting about what is right, or preventing the other from succeeding because we do not want to be proven wrong. Most of us know in our hearts that the problems that exist in America today should not exist. If you agree and agree working together and compromise is "A Better Way" then you are an Optinomic too!

Who can justify hunger in America when we have such an abundance of food? Who can understand the homeless problem as they see building after building being vacated? How do we justify war, hunger and lack of health care to our fellow Americans because we place the importance of money over the loss of lives? What we need to make perfectly clear is that these problems are the results of our insistence upon motivating people to be productive based upon limiting supply. The real problem is that the solution we use to cure our ills is also the cause of them. This is we why can't find lasting solutions. How can we find lasting solutions if we keep using economic policies that cause them?

What we must all realize is that we cannot solve an addition problem by applying the laws of subtraction. You cannot create more by producing less. When it comes to the necessities of life we can produce more than we will ever need or hope to use. Our hunger problem, as we all know, is not due to a lack of food. We have even instituted economic policies that pay farmers not to grow food. Our homeless problem as we know it, has nothing to do with an inability to build homes. Any contractor will build you anything you want. All you need is money. We all know this is true. Since we can't blame the politicians, because after all who is it that elects them, then just what is it that's wrong? What is wrong? In this opinionated world of ours, probably the only thing we all agree on is that something is wrong. The question is not one of what, but why? The answer to this question lies within the economic policies we use today. Economic policies that are Pessinomic in nature! So while it is true that these laws of limited supply were once necessary, they have now reached the point of diminishing return and should no longer be used. The reason why we should no longer use them should be abundantly clear. It is because they are not the cure for the problems we have today, but the cause of them!

This fact is very important, and simply cannot be repeated enough, it is our adherence to limited money supply economics that is the sole reason why we still have most, if not all of the economic problems we suffer today.

Let me ask you this. Do you believe given the modern technologies of today such as food preservation, cloning, hydro farming, crop rotation, and soil preservation that we can provide a sufficient amount of food to feed all Americans, or do you believe as the Pessinomics that some must go hungry so that others may eat? Maybe you believe people must go hungry because we cannot create enough money to buy needed food. It is neither an inability to feed the hungry, nor is it an inability to create the money to buy the food, that is the problem. The problem is intentionally created because we choose to use limited money supply economics to obtain our food.

So I will say it again. Any economic policy in a just society that intentionally limits the obtaining of food, as people go hungry and starve to death should be considered a crime against humanity. How do we justify allowing hunger to exist in this great nation so abundant in food? The problem of course does not only pertain to food. Do you believe we lack the resources to provide adequate housing for all Americans? Perhaps you believe we lack the resources to build and repair our roads and highways, or to manufacture adequate clothing. Just what necessities of life do you believe we cannot provide?

So then why is it we still use limited supply economics? It is because at one time things were much more limited than today and there was no choice, so a policy of limited supply economics made sense. However to continue to adhere to limited money supply economics when that supply is no longer limited, and there is a choice is illogical.

THE CURE IS THE CAUSE!

Understanding limited money supply economics is of the utmost importance. Here is the problem. The same laws of economics that helped produce all the great wonders of the world now prevent the majority of us from obtaining them. So while it is true that in America, any individual or group can become richer, what is also true is that this cannot be done without another group or individual becoming poorer.

Think of 100 people all having one dollar. What happens when through need or desire one of those hundred people give up their dollar? The answer is you now have someone with no dollars. Now unless that person gets that dollar back from the same person to whom it was given, the only way he can get that dollar back is by causing someone else to give up their dollar and be with no dollars. You see if you limit the money supply the only way that someone can have more is by causing another to have less or even none at all.

To better illustrate this point . . . let's take a look at the game called musical chairs. Music is played and when the music stops each player attempts to sit down. The one player who cannot sit down because there is no chair to sit on is out. Now imagine each chair has a dollar on it and you could grab as many dollars as you can as you circled the chairs before the music stopped. How many dollars do you think you would get if you were a bit slower than the rest of the players, or the music stopped with you in between chairs? Does that have anything to do with laziness or a lack of willingness to circle the chairs? No, it doesn't, and so it should be easy to see whenever you limit someone or something must be left out. This also applies to jobs, when there are fewer jobs than there are people, someone can't work.

It would be a wonderful thing if the solution was as simple as adding another chair or more dollars to the chairs. But it is not. We can put $2 on each chair. However, the minute someone gets $4.00, or two people get $3.00, we again have people with $0.00. Neither is the solution a simple matter of limiting the amount a person may obtain. Whether it is inherent or nurtured, some people are just smarter and stronger than others. Because of this, we should never limit productive people who can invent new products, or find cures for disease. It is not in our best interest to do this. We must never take away a person's motivation or curtail their creativity. Since it is a proven fact that incentive for profit motivates people to be productive, to bring out the best in us, we should not only allow people the freedom to pursue and achieve as much wealth as they so desire, we should also encourage it.

DISCOVERING THE
LEMONS!

You can never bake a cherry pie by using lemons as the main ingredients

I can only hope that now you get it . . . . Limiting Leaves Out and The Cure is the Cause. If you don't please re-read what has been written so far over and over again until you do get it. Getting it is the single most important thing that we the people can do. If we truly wish to solve the problems in our economy, there can be no doubt in anyone's mind that we need to do things differently, but where do we begin? Are there some elements in our formula that are undesirable? Are there certain economic common denominators that we have been using for thousands of years that are still being used today? Some common denominators that may be responsible for the economic woes we face. Yes there are, however this now leaves us with some good news and some bad news. The bad news is mankind is a creature of habit and usually resists or is slow to change. If this were not true we would already have made the changes we need. The good news is mankind is also a being endowed with logic, reason and common sense.

Let us now examine the effects of these common denominators, or what I like to call the lemons in the cherry pie of prosperity. For this it seems is the problem. We keep trying to produce a cherry pie of prosperity by using not cherries, but lemons as our main ingredient. Obviously as long as we continue to use lemons as our main ingredient, we can never hope to bake a real cherry pie. Using our powers of observation, are there some historical references to things from which we can draw some conclusions? My observation goes as far back as the history of Rome. We know that there were coins with Caesar's inscription (limited currency). We also know that Joseph and Mary went to Bethlehem to pay their taxes. This leaves two distinct common economic denominators that have existed for at least 2,000 years limited currency and taxes. There are two additional very big lemons that are only about 400 years old . . . the national bank and fractional reserves. The latest lemon is only 100 years old, the Federal Reserve.

What we need is a monetary formula that not only allows us to create money, but one that also allows us to control the quantity of money in circulation in a proper way. Without proper controls only some us will have as much money as we need, but never all of us. Therefore any money supply such as one that is backed by gold or anything else that will limit it, by its very nature will prevent the people who need money the most an ability to get it.

There is also more to the simple controlling of the quantity of money than meets the eye. For example there is the problem of knowing exactly who is it that needs more of that money in circulation, and this is something we can never know, as long as our money supply is limited only to individuals who are determined to be credit worthy by the bank. Those people who do not meet bank standards will not only be denied their desires, they could also be denied the necessities of life as well. These necessities include food, clothing and shelter.

One of the lemons we no longer use is being on a Gold Standard. Many are now advocating putting this lemon back in our recipe. Ponder this, during the panic of 1907 and the great depression and other eras of booms and busts, were we on the gold standard? Was there ever a time that we were on the gold standard that we did not have poverty, inflation and high taxes?

Obviously the gold standard has nothing to due with these things as far as being a cure for their cause. Since by its very nature there is not enough gold to go around to be used as money by all the people, and even if there were, it is an impractical medium of exchange. We should stop wasting our time re-trying something that did not work in the past and impractical to use in the present. Instead we should begin to look for a new and real solution to the monetary system that would best serve the needs of all the people. Also, when referring to good times when we were on the gold standard, no one ever seems to take into account any other factors. Factors like the Gold Rush, the industrial revolution and the increase in immigration providing for cheap labor that causes the loss of American jobs! Does being on the gold standard prevent this? If something was used in the past and it did not work. Is it logical to return to it? I think not, what do you think?

We need to approach creating laws of economics using logic, reason and common sense. What does your logic, reason and common sense tell you about our present economic system? Is it working for all the people? If it is not, then shouldn't our goal be to create a system of economics that does work for all the people?

WHAT IS MONEY?

We can't talk about economics without talking about money, and we can't talk about money unless we all understand exactly what money is and what it does. Money is nothing more than a convenient medium that facilitates the exchange of good and services. Money never has and never will have any intrinsic value. What form of money can be eaten, worn as clothing, or shelter you from the elements? Every practical form of money that man has used has had little or no value until it was spent. If you were on a desert island with millions of dollars or gold bars or silver coins and there was no food for you to eat, you would starve to death.

Money only becomes valuable when you can exchange it for desired goods and services. So I hope this will get those of you trapped on the let's return to gold and silver and a belief that money needs to be backed by something that is limited in order for it to have value carousel, off of it. If a simple limitation of money made it valuable, a law could be quickly passed making it so. Wait a minute that is exactly what we do. We limit the production of money because some economist convinced the people in charge that too much money in circulation made it less valuable, but what if this wasn't true?

Because we now understand that limiting leaves out, we should also understand that any form of money that is limited could never be a solution to our financial problems. It can only perpetuate them. To return to using something that guaranteed we perpetuate a problem is both insane and very foolish, and so is continuing to do something now that perpetuates our problems now both insane and foolish! Don't you agree? Of course if we are going to return to foolish past beliefs, why not also return to believing the Earth is flat and the planets and sun revolve around the Earth.

The only thing that gives money value is the willingness of people to use it. Think about what it is that makes gold and silver valuable? Everyone buys gold and silver to exchange it for . . . money. They buy Gold and Silver hoping it will grow in value. Value to what? Money.

What gives Gold and Silver its value is the exact same thing that gives anything its value, and that is the laws of supply and demand. So while some may want you to think that money is worth less because you could buy an ounce of gold at a much lower price 50 years ago, the truth of the matter is there are simply more people today than in years past. However, compared to the increase in population the quantity of limited precious metals has not equally increased.

Rather than debating a return to the Gold standard we would benefit more from a look at how money is created in the US today. Here is how our present system works. To provide for the needs of the people, our government must either tax us, or borrow from banks at interest, or as it usually does, it will do both. Of course when it borrows from the bank or China! It must raise taxes. It must do this because this is how it gets the money to pay back the lender for its loan. This rise in taxes causes the cost of all goods and services to go up and it creates inflation. This inflation creates the need for additional taxes or more borrowing, which again causes more inflation. We are thus caught in an unending vicious cycle. Because of this it should be crystal clear if we are ever to achieve the real financial stability and prosperity we desire, we must stop this unending vicious cycle.

An alternative to borrowing and increasing taxes is to cut back on needed services. When our government does this, it stops providing for the needs of all the people. Is this what a good government should do? What is the legitimate object of government anyway? Is it to decide that due to a lack of money, that it can easily create, it will provide for the needs of just some of the people, or is it to insure that it provides for the needs of all of the people? Since our Government not only creates political laws, but also creates the economic laws for the people to follow, shouldn't these economic laws allow ALL the people an ability to afford food, clothing, shelter, healthcare, education and all the rest of their needs? Under an equality of law, shouldn't the government ensure that both rich AND poor have equal opportunity to have their needs met?

When a government creates banking laws that allow the rich to increase their wealth with money from loans that are not available to the poor, isn't it then only fair that the government should also create laws that allow the poor to increase their wealth with money not available to the rich? Since the real purpose of our banking system should be to create wealth for all the people. Perhaps we would be better served if our banks loaned money based upon a person's need rather than their ability to repay the loan with interest!

What I find illogical is why we allow the banks to be the wealth and money creators in the first place. What I find even more amazing is how many people are unaware that our Government does not create nor control our money supply. It is the independent banks that make up the Federal Reserve System that control both the quantity and the distribution of our money. Since the government is not creating the money then what is it that gives these Federal Reserve notes their value? Oddly enough, it's our government's approving them as legal tender.

When even a great economist such as Milton Friedman doesn't seem to know that the Federal

Reserve System is as Federal as Federal Express and that it is not part of the Government and has never been part of the Government. We are all in serious trouble.

You may not believe what follows but when the federal government is in need of money what does it do? It prints up bonds, which are a promise to pay a loan with interest. Let's say this amount is for $1,000,000,000. The government then gives these bonds to the Federal Reserve. The Federal Reserve then authorizes the US mint to print $1,000,000,000 dollars in Federal Reserve Notes and deposit that money into the treasury. Of course today this is all done electronically. But as you can see, these Federal Reserve notes are not backed up by anything of value other than the government's stamp of approval and promise to make good on paying the bonds.

Since this is new money printed by the US mint and does not come from money banks already have on hand, isn't this actually our own (Government's) money? If it is our money, what exactly is it that the banks are lending to us and why are we paying them interest to do it?

Oddly enough this is only one of the ways that our present banking laws allows The Federal Reserve to create money to their benefit and not ours. There is a second way that they can do it, and it's called fractional reserves. Fractional reserves allow the banks to grant loans equaling up to ten times or more than they actually have in their vault! Here's the problem with this. If debt is created without creating both the principle and interest to repay it, how can that debt and interest be repaid? It can't, and so default is imminent. Because of the laws of limited supply to avoid default you must either cause another to have less, thereby causing default by another, or you must again borrow from the bank! Good for banks, but not for people!

At present the only way our government can add money into an expanding economy is to tax the people, or for Congress to authorize bonds (debt) to be created. Since most money is transferred electronically, what if Congress could simply authorize a direct deposit of that $1,000.000,000, or for that matter any amount of credits needed by it into the treasury. Wouldn't that make more sense, be more logical, and be the more reasonable thing to do? Why borrow money with interest added to pay for something later, when we can just pay for it now without interest. If we did, we would never have to repay the Federal Reserve back at interest on money it never had, nor would we have any deficit to pass onto future generations. We also would not have to worry about the government shutting down or not being able to pay its debt, because there would be no debt. Since the government can now simply deposit the credits it needs into the treasury, there also would be no need to tax the people to raise the funds the government needed to provide for the common defense and promote the general welfare.

Upon reading the Constitution, which is the law of the land, we find it gives the authorization, power, and an implied obligation for Congress to coin money and regulate the amount of that money! Since Congress has the power to create wealth (money), why does it choose to let the banks do this, and then borrow it from them at interest? Is that logical to you?

What we need are economics that work for all the people. We also need the government and its money back in the hands of the people to insure that this happens. We also need to amend the Federal Reserve Act so that banks may only lend their own money, not ours, and disallow the practice of fractional reserves.

When it comes to the creation and distribution of the wealth of this nation, we remain somehow mysteriously bound to outdated methods and economic policies that defy logic, reason, and common sense. What we need are ideas based on a methodology that will eradicate the cause of the very real problems that still exist here in the United States.

INFLATION

When talking about laws of economics used to produce money, we must always consider the effects of inflation. There are only two real causes for inflation. They are increased costs and limited supply. Since money is presently being used as the motivating factor for the production of goods and services, the use of a limited money supply can only result in limiting the production of goods and services. When this is done we cause the demand to become higher than the supply and inflation is created. This inflation by demand also allows only some of the people to obtain products or services by making it impossible for others to obtain them. Again, with old world economics this is purposely done to drive the price up to make it more profitable so that the goods or services provider has motivation to create them.

There also appears to some, to be two types of money supply inflation. The first of this type of inflation is caused by a lack of money and therefore prevents the supply from being created to meet the needs of the people. The other, some believe, is caused when too much money is in supply. I wonder who would want us to believe that too much money and not a lack of money is a bad thing? Who gets hurt most when there is too much money in the system and who is it that benefits most from a shortage of money? Does a banker make more money when there is a shortage of money or an abundance of money? Do more people borrow money when there is a shortage of money or an abundance of money? Does the government borrow when it has a shortage of money or an abundance of money? If I were a banker able to create money and collect profits in the form of loan fees and interest, I would prefer that people believe less money and not more money is a good thing. After all, who wouldn't like to have less money? I wouldn't how about you?

Personally I don't buy into the theory that just because people have money they are willing to pay more. Also in a competitive fair market economy, if a merchant is inflating their prices, and there is sufficient money in the economy, competition will be created and the price of an item will come down. Also inflation of this type caused by too much money in circulation really doesn't matter, because having sufficient money to buy the things you need or want at a higher price is better than not having money to buy items you can't buy at a lower price.

Since a major cause of inflation is increased costs, if the government needs to pay the interest on a loan and decides to raise that money by taxing the people, when the people pay that tax to maintain their standard of living they must somehow replace that money, if they want to keep their standard of living. Listed below are three ways to do it:

The first way is to personally work harder and longer or to have your family join the job market. That's what's happening today. However in a limited job market, when families are forced to work harder, other families are denied an ability to work at all. Many people find it easier to put the blame on people for this, rather than blame the economy. However in a limited supply economy where jobs are limited, whenever given a choice, an employer will always choose the better worker. Because we are human beings who are not all created physically and mentally equal, human beings who get sick, and grow older and weaker, whether we choose to or not, there is no way we can forever be that best worker, nor keep that competitive edge.

Unfortunately people who cannot work are still part of the demand side of the equation. Through no fault of their own, they are now not part of the supply side. You may continue to delude yourself into thinking that those who are unemployed simply don't want to work. This however denies the real problem, which is our present law of limited supply economics! If you are unemployed perhaps you once thought people just didn't want to work too! Do you still feel the same way today?

Think about it. If everybody who supposedly doesn't want to work was to wake tomorrow and look for a job, where are the jobs? What we are talking about are real jobs and not minimum wage jobs. Just how many of us would be happy or even able to pay our bills on a job that paid minimum wage? Imagine if we could make it a requirement for Congress to live on minimum wage and without health insurance for their term of office! If we could do this, how fast do you think things would change then?

The government now unable to get tax money from the unemployed, and lacking the funds to create more jobs, the government must once again look to the working person for more money and institute yet another tax increase.

A second way to replace the money needed would be to cut back on buying certain goods and services. Many Americans are now forced to do this. However this too results in putting people out of work. If a company can't make a profit because they can't sell the products they have on the shelf, that company certainly won't employ more people to produce goods and services they can't sell. This causes employers to cutback on production and that causes a spiraling of job loses. Also going without what you once could afford immediately lowers your standard of living.

The third way you could make up that missing money is to ask for a raise. We all know what happens when this is done. That raise is passed along to the consumer and again there is inflation. Also each time there are increased costs, not only do we pay a higher price for goods and services, which cuts into our wealth and make the dollar less valuable. This increase in costs also causes the government, which was paying less for an item, to now pay a higher price for it.

The government is now in need, once again, of more money. Where does it go for the money? It goes back to the working person who now must give up more of his money. How does he do that? He has three ways, he can work harder and longer and . . . do you get the picture?

As if this is not bad enough, it gets worse. Whenever there is an increase in costs, the selling price almost always goes beyond the actual increase. For example, if it costs $1.00 to produce something, and a businessman determines he wants a 25% return on his investment, the selling price would be $1.25. For the purpose of simple analogy what happens when through taxation, we add an additional dollar to that cost? Two factors come into play. First, does that businessman keep the same markup with more capital at risk? That is highly unlikely. However, even if he does, 25% of $2.00 (the new cost to produce) is $2.50, not $2.25. Once this is understood, the choice becomes simple. We must either amend or repeal the income tax amendment, or experience never-ending inflation. Once this is understood, what are our choices? The answer is simple, we must either amend or repeal the income tax amendment, or experience never-ending inflation.

THE FIRST LEMON . . . TAXES

Now let's see if you understand the problem! What will happen if we do not amend or repeal the income tax amendment? Since what we all want is to be as wealthy as we so desire, and for some that means unlimited wealth. Our new economic formula cannot include either an income tax or sales tax. Wealth should never be curtailed, as this is counterproductive. If this is so, then how can wealth be logically taxed? Taxes burden, slow down, limit. That is the nature of a tax. How can we achieve unlimited wealth if we use policies that limit it? We can't, because that's what taxing and limiting means!

What really boggles my mind is that even though it is so easy to see that taxes are the cause, and not the cure for our economic problems. We insist upon not only keeping them, but we also allow them to continually rise. Why is it that we have repealed prohibition but will not repeal the Income Tax Amendment even though the reason for its creation is no longer an issue? What makes matters worse is that there is now undeniable proof that the 16th

Amendment was accepted as law as a result of fraud and in direct violation of the Constitution. With that in mind one would think that the Supreme Court would strike the law as unconstitutional! Where's our system of checks and balances?

To understand why this amendment was needed, you should first know that before 1913 there was no income tax in America. Well that's not entirely true. President Lincoln did tax income to fund the Civil War. He also issued more paper money for the same purpose. However generally speaking, before 1913 there was no Income Tax.

This means from 1776 to 1913 the government supported itself and provided for goods and services without the help of an income tax. That means for 137 years our nation survived without the need for the 16th Amendment. It was also during this time that we experienced one the greatest growth and eras of prosperity in our nation's history. This was prompted by the gold rush and industrial revolution that saw our money supply dramatically increase. That's one and half times as long without an income tax than as with it. It must also be understood that this was also a direct result of an increase in government revenue through new gold and silver discoveries. Just exactly did all the people with this new gold do? They traded their gold for guess what? Money!

To truly understand the reasons for creating the income tax we must take a good look at the history of the world in 1913. There was a war in Europe and the world was on the Gold Standard. The allies having used their own limited supply of gold and silver for their own war effort were now in need of the gold and silver in our treasury to continue that war effort.

However since being on the Gold Standard meant that all our gold was backing our paper money in circulation. There was no gold available to loan to our European allies. At this same time America was also changing from an agricultural nation to an industrialized one. Now here is where the laws of limited supply come into play. The paper in circulation was limited to the gold and silver on reserve. The gold and silver was limited to what could be mined or received from another country through trade. At this time the gold rush was over and we already had most of the Gold and Silver of the allies.

Since we know that limiting leaves out. Spear headed by the war what began to happen was the paper money previously used to buy agricultural products was now being used to buy the products being produced by the factories. This caused a problem for the farmer who was now receiving less of the limited monetary supply. This also caused the price of food to rise and with it good old circular inflation. When the cost of food rises, since it is a basic need of life, everyone needs more money to meet this need. Naturally what follows is for wages to go higher. When that happens, we see a rise in the cost of all goods and services. At this time the farmer was still a very large and influential political group, so the politicians of the day were very sympathetic to their problems.

What takes place next is nothing more than good old American ingenuity. In steps the Income Amendment to the rescue. By allowing the government to tax the income of the people and thereby force them to give some of the paper in circulation back to the government, the government was able to kill two birds with one stone.

The paper in the treasury now allowed the government to use some of that money to subsidize the farmer, and some of that money could go towards helping the allies' war effort. When the war ended, it would have been prudent to now repeal the Income Tax Amendment, as it was no longer needed. This of course was never done. It seems to me to be an odd coincidence that both the Income Tax Amendment and the Federal Reserve Act were enacted in 1913.

It also seems strange to me that it has taken 100 years before we are connecting the dots, and first beginning to realize that it was rival bankers acting together that put all this into play. By combining these two laws together the banking community was able to virtually lend Congress whatever money it needed. It also guaranteed these loaned would be repaid to them by authorizing the Congress to tax the income of the people. Best of all they got to do it all without putting up any money of their own!

What I find very strange is that every time we go to war our economic policies of limitation seem to go out the window. If remaining on a limited money supply were better for the production of goods and services, why does the government in times of war always go off such policies? What I also find very strange and illogical is any need for creating such things as bonds or any other financial instrument to obtain money, when the government has the authority to produce all the money it needs. Once again why are we borrowing, if we don't need to do so? From whom are we borrowing and where is the lender getting the money to give to us? Certainly the consequence of simply adding more money to a needed economy cannot be more harmful than borrowing to do it. The mere fact that there is a need to borrow indicates that more money is needed. So adding that money has to be better than not adding it to the economy, and adding it debt free has to be better for the country than needing to pay back a loan with interest.

Since money is nothing more than a median of exchange to facilitate the production of goods and services, and if what makes a nation sovereign is the ability to create that median of exchange? Why are so many countries in debt to the detriment of their own people? Also why do they keep insisting upon continuing to produce that median of exchange through a banking system and debt, rather than simply producing money on their own? In a free market if a country were to have goods and services valued by other countries, their money would be desired. So once again I ask the question why do sovereign nations borrow from banks their own money and then not only give that money back to the banks but add interest to it too!

Now a logical mind that can reason and use its common sense would have to ask, why do this, and who is it that benefits from doing so? Certainly not the people who must bear the increased tax burden needed to pay not only the interest on this non-loan, but who must also pay back the non-loan too. Neither does their burden stop there! They also must now deal with the inflation that is caused by business and governments' need to pay for this increase in costs caused by the increase in taxes. Talking about insanity, what is this law of economics all about anyway? The simple truth is that our laws of economics are not designed for the benefit the people, they are designed for the benefit of the bankers who created them.

THE PROPER RECIPE!

What do you think would happen, if we did amend or repeal the income tax amendment? First of all the government would need to change the laws of economics that funds its programs, and that would be a good thing. The time for change is now. We are not in need of new laws of economics. We are in desperate need of new laws of economics. New laws of economics that are not designed to redistribute the wealth of America, but new laws of economics that will distribute the new wealth of America in a new way. We also must guarantee that this new system must not be one that allows some to have by causing others to have less, or not at all.

Here's a thought! What if instead of using a complicated tax and banking system to put money into circulation and to provide for the common good, the government simply paid the army, navy, air force, marines all federal employees and all of its programs. What if those programs included all those in need, such as the ill, the elderly, the costs of education and the costs of health-care? The people receiving this money being in need of goods and services would go to the merchants and make their purchases. If more money was needed in circulation, we could increase federal payments or create new worthwhile government projects.

An alternate way of adding more money into the economy could be by way of an income bonus. This bonus could be given to our merchants if they hired more people or lowered the price of their goods and services. If too much money was deemed in circulation, we could institute an inflation tax. At least then we would be using taxes in a proper way. That is to limit. This certainly makes more sense to me than the raising and the lowering of an interest rate by a person not even voted into office. Does any of this make sense to you? Because I am Optinomic I am convinced that there are many different ways we could use to create the wealth of America in "A Better Way".

However, before any economic reform can be created, we must first proactively seek it out. If you want a real economic stimulus, a good place to start would be to repeal the Income Tax Amendment. Practically speaking, what do you think would happen if people were to have more money? Let's say the amount presently paid in income taxes! It would be like the great gold rush all over again and a transfusion of wealth into the economy

There are only two things that we can do with money and they are to either spend it now, or you can save it and spend it later. If we spend it now, what would happen? Money spent now would create the "trickle up" effect. When there are no more products or services for the American businessman to sell, if he believes he will make a profit, the American businessman will create more goods and services. He'll do this without a single tax incentive from the government. Making a profit is the only incentive any businessman needs. Besides, why put the money in the hands of somebody "up there" and wait for it to trickle down here, when down here is where you really want it in the first place? It would appear that for most people the "trickle up" effect is better than a trickle down one.

If the people were to save their money instead of spending it, the banks would then have more money to lend. Borrowed money is never saved. It always buys something, and that can create both the trickle up and the trickle down effect. If we had no taxes at all on our dollar, we would have nothing limiting or burdening it. We would have a true dollar. Unencumbered, the natural law of supply and demand may eventually be able to use that invisible hand discussed by Adam Smith in his book "Wealth of a Nation". Until it does, I suggest we use the visible hand of the Federal Government to point us in the right direction.

Now I am sure that there will be those who will claim that this will cause inflation. To this I say would it, and if it did, would it really matter? As previously stated, who cares about the cost of an item as long as you have the money to buy that item? Sure beats not having the money to buy what you need or want, right? Plus, if products can be produced at a profit for less than they are selling for now, in a FREE Market economy new businesses will arise creating competition, and competition causes the price of goods and services to fall. Finally if all else failed, we could institute an inflation tax to keep prices in check.

Which is the proper recipe to bake an economic cherry pie for all? Is the proper recipe one that includes an ingredient that only allows some to have, or have more by causing others to have less, or not at all, or should it be one that uses an ingredient that allows some to have or have more, without causing another to have less, or not at all? Should we continue to be unable to bake our cherry pie because we keep using the ingredient of taxes that limit one's wealth and perpetuate inflation, or should we eliminate such an ingredient from our recipe? Should we continue to be unable to bake our cherry pie because we keep using the ingredient of limited distribution that prevents available resources from reaching the people, such as an abundance of food from being able to reach the hungry, or should such an ingredient be eliminated?

What do you think? I think we should eliminate from our recipe any ingredient that stops an abundance of food from feeding the hungry. Don't you agree? Should we use ingredients that allow our government to provide for needs of its people, or should we to use ingredients that prevent it from doing so? Which should we choose?

To bake a real cherry pie of prosperity we need to do three simple things. First we must eliminate the ingredients that make it impossible to create our cherry pie. Next we must add the ingredients that will bake that cherry pie. Finally we must bake the ingredients using the proper recipe, and the proper recipe is a Constitutional Democracy.

DEMOCRACY THE LOGICAL CHOICE!

There were many reasons for the American Revolution. We all are aware of the Colonist fight against taxes. With slogans such as "taxation without representation is tyranny" the birth of a new nation began. What then could be said of those political leaders who get themselves elected with the promise of lower taxes or even no new taxes?

Since taxes virtually always increase, are these politicians simply guilty of lying or are they guilty of tyranny? How can we have a representative government if the representatives refuse to represent? How do we practice Democracy without giving to each one of us not only a vote, but also a vote that counts?

We are all taught in school about the Boston Tea party, however how many of us know what Benjamin Franklin cited as the prime cause of the Revolution? According to Benjamin Franklin, "The refusal of King George to allow the colonies to operate an honest monetary system, which freed the common man from the clutches of the money manipulators was probably the prime cause of the Revolution." Isn't it curious that this is not taught in our schools, can you wonder why?

Democracy, what a novel ideal! An ideal based on the premise that all men are created equal and therefore are entitled to an equal say in the decisions that affect them. Democracy, a belief in majority rule with guaranteed rights to the minority. One that allows the minority, if it can by lawful means to itself become the majority. Democracy, it's the one and only ideal to applaud the fundamental dignity and worth of each individual. Democracy, that always alluded to but never truly practiced philosophy.

To create a government based upon democratic principles, our forefathers risked their fortunes and their lives. They challenged and defeated the greatest power of their day. They literally changed the world. Once again in the course of human events, we find ourselves in a revolting situation. However, what we need to do today is not revolt, but EVOLVE. We need to take our representative government to what the founding fathers truly desired. If we look at early America, we will find that Democracy was much closer to being practiced than the so-called Democracy practiced in America today.

In early America problems and answers were brought to town meetings where the people made their wishes known. Their elected representative then went to Washington and literally voted as per the wishes of the town. In effect, each person's wishes or vote was counted. Today we elect officials based upon their promise to do something, which more often than not this promise is not upheld. We also vote not to re-elect a representative based upon how they voted in the past. This is pretty much like closing the barn after all the animals ran away. To continue to do this does not honor our forefathers, it mocks them. To truly honor our forefathers, we must finish the work they had begun.

If Americans truly love Democracy, then why do we fear becoming a nation that is truly Democratic? Why? It is because those few who are in power do not want to be subjected to the will of the people. They will distort the tenants of Democracy to explain it to their own gain. They will tell you that Democracy is bad because if the majority of the people wish to kill the minority they can. This is far from the truth because Democracy guarantees not only the rights of the majority but it also guarantees those of the minority as well. It even allows for the minority to become the majority by lawful means.

If we are to properly compare a Republic to Democracy we need to either compare a Republic, which is an Oligarchy (rule by the few) to a Democracy (rule by the majority) or we must compare a Constitutional Republic to a Constitutional Democracy. It is the Constitution (rule by law) that is the important part. Today we subscribe to a Constitutional Republic form of government. Today laws that were never debated or brought to the people for their approval like the Patriot Act that takes away precious freedoms guaranteed in the Constitution, and laws allowing the ruling few to shut down the Internet if they so desire have been turned into law. However, I wonder if we were ruled as a Democratic Republic and the people could vote on these laws, if they ever would have been passed?

There are those who also argue that to be a Republic is better than being a Democracy because a good speaker may sway the people. Their logic is that some 350,000,000 plus Americans can be fooled easier than 535 people, the Representatives and Senators that make up our Congress. Representatives and Senators who more often than not show their allegiance, not to the people that elected them, but to the corporations and the party that supports them.

Does that sound logical to you? Also since a simple majority of the Congress in most cases is all that is needed to pass and enact laws. The real number of people ruling this country is closer to only 268 or 350 people if you take into consideration the number of people it takes to over ride a presidential veto. How in the world does someone argue that this is democracy or rule by a majority of the people? What do you think? Is it easier to repeatedly influence 350 Congressmen and Senators with millions of dollars in campaign funds and other perks to allow an illogical, unreasonable, non sensible procedure to continue, or is it easier to convince 350,000,000 plus

Americans that they should pay taxes so the banks can create our money and select who gets it?

If this is not enough to convince you that a Democratic Republic is better than Representative Republic, I have no idea what will! For all those who still fear the swaying of the people is easier than the controlling of the Congress, we also have a FREE press, our Constitution and our system of checks and balances. Today we also have the Internet.

As a Representative Republic, the people have the right and opportunity to vote for who shall decide the outcome of the issues that affect them. In a Democratic Republic the people have a choice. They can either allow their Representative to vote on the issue or they can exercise their right to decide on the outcome of an issue for themselves.

I say let the people decide if it is better to produce our own money and have no need for taxes to provide the goods and services that we need and desire. If they were given this choice as opposed to letting the banks continue to run the show, which one do you think the people will choose? Allowing our Government to create our money and control its quantity is the only right and proper thing to do! I almost can't wait to hear the illogical and nonsensical rhetoric that must be invented to defend our present system.

Because of the technology of today we really have no need for taxes at all. The only exceptions might be an inflation tax to keep prices in check, or a discouragement tax to dissuade people from things deemed harmful such as drinking alcohol and smoking cigarettes. Using today's digital technology the government could simply add whatever amount of credits needed to fund all of its programs to the US treasury. Credits that can be further transferred to wherever needed for programs such as homeland security, and national defense. Unlimited credits that can buy armor not for just some, but for all of our servicemen and women. Unlimited credits for programs such as job assurance (not unemployment insurance), Social Security, Medicare, Medicaid, education, and all the needs this country may have and can produce, but presently doesn't produce due to a lack of money.

If it were true that when businesses have more money they would create more jobs, can you image how many new jobs will be created if companies would be free of both individual and businesses taxes! If it is also true as professed by believers in the trickle up theory that by giving money to the people to buy the products being produced by business would cause job creation, one could only imagine how well companies would treat their employees with all of these new jobs competing for workers. Not only jobs and job security would be created, but this relief from paying taxes is sure to create a higher standard of living for all Americans.

Whether you believe in the trickle up theory or the trickle down theory, we must come together and demand that our Congress not only exercise its authority to coin money and regulate the quantity thereof, we must also remind our representatives that in taking an oath to uphold and defend the Constitution that they have the obligation to do so for the benefit of all the people.

Along with our understanding that limiting leaves out, it should be just as easy to understand that we can never be truly represented on all matters that concern us by using limited representation. How long do we need to be trapped in the 18th century? How have the problems of poverty, unemployment, taxes, and crime improved since then? We have had rule, as a Republic for many years, how is that working out? How well do you feel represented? If the people are to ever have the power to rule and to achieve the economic and political goals that we truly desire, we must first achieve a Constitutional Democracy and the sooner we do it the better. This truth is self-evident

As a direct result of the Internet technology of today, we can finally achieve something we have been unable to do. That is we can create a true Constitutional and Democratic Republic. Becoming a Democratic Republic is the only way to insure that our representatives must vote as per the wishes of their constituents, and not a political party, lobbyists, or in their own best interests.

Who can deny that today it seems that our Congress is more concerned with spending money and putting

Americans lives at risk in some foreign country, than they are interested in putting money into healthcare and education here at home. Do you believe the majority of Americans agrees with spending money abroad over spending money at home, or giving FREE healthcare and other services to illegal aliens, or that they would vote for such a thing!

So then what is the logical conclusion? The logical conclusion is our government is not of, by, and for the people as it should be. Today it seems our government is all about the money! Who benefits the most from remaining a Republic even though we can be a Democracy and have majority rule? Who is it that is really making the rules? Think about who is in control of the money today! Who do you think it is? Is it the people, or is it the bankers and CEO's of large corporations? What the occupiers call the 1%. Is that rule by the majority, or is that rule by an oligarchy?

Today we can practice true Democracy, and only a true Democracy can be of, by, and for the people. Of this you can be certain, when the few make the laws, they will not care about what will benefit the minority, or about what benefits the majority of the people. They will only care about what benefits them.

Once again I ask the question, who is the best person to vote on the laws that effect you? Is it you or others? Using the communication technology that we have today, it is now possible for all Americans to be informed of the issues, debate the issues, and vote on the issues faster than it took our founding fore-fathers to get from where they lived to Washington.

Here is the very real problem of a representative government. It is also undeniable proof why no one but you can truly represent you on all the issues. To clarify, let us assume the following:

Candidate A is For	Candidate B is For	The People Are
Taxes	No Taxes	80% No Taxes
No Free Health Care	Free Health Care	80% Free Health Care
No Abortion	Abortion	70% No Abortion

Given the issues are of equal importance Candidate B is most likely to be elected. However when it comes to voting on the issue of abortion he is going to vote not only against your wishes but also against the wishes of the majority of the people. Plus there is no guarantee that just because a candidate says he is for an issue or against it, that he will vote as he proclaimed. Do you see the problem? We have had rule, as a Republic for many years and once again I ask you, how well is that working out? How can we practice rule by the majority, when those who get elected are no longer subjected to the will of the people, or must vote how they said they would vote.

Now some may argue that the people won't vote on all issues, and that is okay as long as they have that choice. I believe that the main reason people are not voting is because they believe their vote won't count, or there isn't any real choice. Just like with our economics, our ability to achieve Representative Democracy has changed. There are also many ways to motivate people to vote. What if people were rewarded for voting and taxed for not voting? I am sure if we pose this question to the American people, they will come up with many satisfactory ways to get people to vote.

To love Democracy and not practice it is illogical. I think we can also all agree that it is illogical for America to have a hunger problem amidst our abundance of food. I would now like to address how illogical are the economic rules for business we use today.

Here's what we say, "Mr. Businessman to be successful in America, you need to adhere to the following 5 Rules:

Rule #1, use the cheapest products to produce goods and services.

Rule #2, employ the least amount of people that you can to do this.

Rule #3, pay those employed people the least that you can.

Rule #4, sell you goods and services for the most that you can and

Rule #5, hide as much profit as you can from the government.

Like or not, these are the rules as developed in the 18th century still followed today. If this is Capitalism is there any wonder why people dislike it? Do you really believe that this is the best way to produce goods and services for the betterment of all the people?

Here is my dilemma. Are doing things that defy, logic, reason and common sense "A Better Way? Now don't get me wrong, I am not against the fundamentals of Capitalism or a free market economy, just the contrary. What I am against is any economic system that may have been logical for the time period for which it was created, but is not logical today. I believe we need a new and improved economic system based on the fundamentals of capitalism and a FREE market economy, but one that is in line with 21st century technology.

With that in mind, I submit the following.

Concerning Rule #1, if it is preferable to buy quality products, how can the use of an economic formula that motivates companies to create the cheapest product possible be logical?

As for Rule #2, if full employment is our goal, how can we achieve this by economic laws that motivate a company profits more by using the fewest people possible?

Now as for Rule # 3, if we desire for the people to achieve wealth and to have higher standard of living, how can this be achieved by economic laws that motivate a business to pay employees the least that it can? Also if people have more money to buy goods and services, would that not create a trickle up economy and stimulate the businessman to create more goods and services?

As for Rule# 4, if we desire to make quality products affordable to all, how do we logically conclude it is better to use economic rules that motivate companies to make more by selling to the public for the most they can as opposed to making it more profitable for companies to sell their goods and services for the least that they can? Can we do that? Of course we can! We now have the technology to make it easy to do.

As for Rule# 5, how do we argue that it is logical to include an income or sales tax when creating economic rules for creating profit and wealth? Taxes limit or burden. That is what they are by definition.

Let's pretend for a moment that on the ballot are the 2 sets of rules below. Which seems more logical to you?

Present Set of Rules

Rule# 1 Motivate a business to create the cheapest products

Rule# 2 Motivate a business to hire the fewest people they can.

Rule# 3 Motivate a business to pay employees the least they can.

Rule# 4 Motivate a business to sell at highest price that they can

Rule# 5 Motivate a business to show the least they can, if they don't the government will take away as much as it can.

Optinomic Set of Rules

Rule# 1 Motivate a business to create the best products possible

Rule# 2 Motivate a business to hire the most people that they can.

Rule# 3 Motivate a business to pay employees the most they can.

Rule# 4 Motivate a business to sell at lowest price that they can

Rule# 5 Motivate our businessmen to show as much business as they can because we the government will reward them for it.

Can these Optinomic Rules be achieved? Yes they can, and as we continue we will discuss new programs we can quickly create and implement to achieve them.

A MATTER OF COMMON SENSE!

We all know our policies are not working or at the very least are not working for all. However, before we attempt to fix something, we should understand how it works and why it is broken.

To do this, we must understand certain principles such as cause, effect and motivation. It is also important to use our powers of observation. Once it is understood that the cure is the cause, that the economic laws that we use today to solve our problems are what causes them. It then becomes very easy to understand why we have the illogical problems that face us today.

It is this new understanding that brings us to our first decision? Should we remain a nation that insists we continue to follow failure proven Pessinomic (negative resulting for the majority) policies of the past, or do we develop new Optinomic (positive resulting for all) policies for the future? What do you think? Should we? I think we should.

This takes us to this next question. Is it really possible to create such Optinomic policies, or are they beyond our capability too difficult to achieve? When compared to the rest of the technology we have created, this should be a simple task. All we need to do to create them is to use our logic, reason and common sense.

Economic policies are not God given. They are created and followed by man. As such they can be voted in, they can be voted out, and they can produce any number of results. To better understand the results we are getting, we must first let us look at the choices we are making.

One of our choices has been to produce nothing, as is the case with our present unemployment and most of our entitlement programs. If the main law of our economic formula is to create a supply to be greater than the demand! Logic dictates we need all who can be productive to be productive.

Another policy we could choose to follow is one that creates an inadequate supply. Such a policy would create for example, 50 cars for 100 people. It should be easy to see that no matter how hard we try all 100 people cannot have one car each. If the example was 50 meals, or 50 jobs for 100 people, a policy of inadequate supply is easily seen as undesirable and something that we must change, right?

Now this is very important. Whether you actually produce less or limit the money supply, the results are the same as if you never produced the product in the first place. This is because it is only possible for some of the people to obtain what's needed or desired, but never all of the people. Nor does it matter what it is . . . food, shelter, clothing, jobs, healthcare, education and everything else are all limited by a limited money supply. So it should be very easy to see why a policy causing results such as this is very undesirable and one of the very first things that we need to change.

A third policy we can create would produce an adequate supply, limited by distribution. This is what our present banking practices cause to happen and why they must be changed! Who has access to the new money created? It certainly is not the unemployed man on the street desperately in need of money. Have you ever tried to borrow money when you were unemployed? Trust me, it's not going to happen. A simple explanation of adequate supply limited by distribution can be best illustrated by using the example of 100 cars for 50 people. This does not mean each person gets 2 cars. Depending upon how the wealth is distributed, one person could have it all, he could buy all 100 cars. This would leave the others without any cars.

Hence a supply of food is unable to meet the demand by the people, although adequate to feed them. With this policy the problem of limitation is in the distribution of money rather than in the money supply. Think about how we create and distribute our money and it should become very easy to understand why we have the problems for the 99% that we do.

When using rules of economics such as this, it is of little help for most people. This is because of their inability to obtain some of the new money and wealth created. It should therefore be easy to see why using a rule of economics that prevent the majority of people from obtaining new wealth is also undesirable.

Our government today administers and fosters some form of all three of these economic policies. However, because of today's technology, there is now another group of economic policies that we can choose to follow. They are Optinomic in nature and would create an adequate money supply not limited by distribution, but instead enhanced by it.

It should be the duty of an economist to seek out such Optinomic policies that eliminate the "lack of" goods and services. A good economist would create wealth, or at least the ability to achieve it for all the people. To do this, an economic policy must create a supply that is greater than its demand. To achieve this, an economist must know what motivates people to be productive. If not, who needs an economist whose philosophy is to have us do without, or an economic formula that motivates people to be non-productive?

To reap the real rewards of economics it should be treated as a science and not a philosophy. Whenever performing any scientific investigation there are laws of cause and effect. There is also an observance of whether a formula is working or not working. Observe the results of the economic formulas followed today. What are your observations? What are your conclusions? How well do the economic formula we use today work for all the people? Are they Optinomic or Pessinomic? Do they produce positive or negative results for the majority of the people?

THE 2ND LEMON-THE FEDERAL RESERVE!

As evidenced by his later remarks President Woodrow Wilson when signing the Federal Reserve Act into law had no idea of how the Federal Reserve System would truly work, or the harm it could cause. It's also a shame that he did not realize this until after it was too late.

Be that as it may, as long as we continue to allow the banking cartel to be in charge of the control of the supply of our money, instead of the government or the people, it is the bankers who will determine who gets the money they need and who doesn't.

Just like returning to a gold standard is not in our best interest and is one of those economic tools that have proven not to be a solution for the poverty, shortage of jobs and other ails of our society. So too, the Federal Reserve has also proven itself to be one of those economic tools that we use today to solve our problems that not only does not provide the solution that we seek, but is also one of the underlying causes of the problems we have today.

The Federal Reserve does not control inflation nor does it guarantee the security of a monetary system as intended. Instead it actually creates inflation because of the interest it charges the government. This causes more taxes to be needed and this in turn causes the cost of good to rise. Plus if our unnecessary borrowing from banks were eliminated, there would be no national debt. Also without accountability as to what the Banks of the Federal Reserve can or cannot do, there can never be any guarantee that our money supply will be stabile. This is because the present Federal Reserve Act allows a small group of people to determine what is best for our country. If that is not in line with what is best for them, you can be sure that without any accountability, they will choose what is best for them over what's best for the country every time. After seeing the Federal Reserve System in actual operation for nearly 100 years? Is the present Federal Reserve Act a solution to our problems, or a cause of them?

Since not everything about the Federal Reserves is bad, what should we do with it? While allowing the government to borrow money at interest or even at all needs to be changed. The present system in place for record keeping, making public loans, moving money from place to place and performing electronic transfers does not need changing. Since the Federal Reserve System already has all of this in place, dissolving it does not seem to be in our best interest. While we definitely need to change those things within an economic formula that need to be changed. We should not fix what is not broken. Don't you agree?

In his lecture on the greatest financial myths Dr. Friedman claims that the depression was a failure of Government and not big business. While Dr. Friedman is right in all his explanations as to what the Federal Reserve did wrong, especially their refusal to pump money into a depressed economy, he seemed to have forgotten or has been fooled like most of the people into believing that the Federal Reserve is part of the U.S. Government.

The real truth of the matter is it is not now, nor was it ever a part of our Federal Government. It is now and has always been part of big business, and neither the President nor the Congress has any power over the policies of the Federal Reserve. It is also true, that if FDR did not institute public works programs, take us off the Gold Standard, and cause more money to be pumped into the economy, who knows how long the Great Depression would have continued?

What most Americans do not realize is that all the banks that constitute the Federal Reserve are privately owned. What is also true is that through their member banks the Federal Reserve has caused, does cause and will continue to cause the booms, depressions and recessions as they see fit. The reason why they do this is because the business of business is business and these are the things that allow banks to make a profit. So if you believe that these economic booms and busts have anything to do with what's best for the people or the country, you are sadly mistaken. To the banks of the Federal Reserve it is only business.

Yes as Dr. Friedman said, "It is the Federal Reserve that is solely responsible for the Depression" . . . and for the inflation imposed upon us. It is imposed upon us not only by the rise in the cost of goods and services, but it is also imposed upon us directly from the government needing to tax us to pay both the debt and the interest that the Federal Reserve charges us. A debt with interest that just keeps growing and growing. Yes! You're right again Dr. Friedman; the Constitution does give the government the right to coin money and to regulate its value. So why doesn't it?

Remember what we have to do to get the money to pay for things that we cannot afford. We have previously discussed 3 ways. There is of course a fourth way and that is to borrow the needed money. However if we do this, we now must pay the principle due and the added the interest too, and if you recall, the money to pay this interest is never created and thus made impossible to be repaid. The truth of the matter is simply this. You cannot borrow your way out of debt, anymore than you can drink yourself sober. So let's take the power to coin money out of the hands of the bankers and put it back in the hands of the people.

WOULD YOU IF YOU COULD?

The obvious question is this, are we abundant or limited? There is no doubt that we are blessed to live in one of the most abundant nations on Earth. It is this abundance however, that also confuses us. How is it possible to believe or understand a hunger problem in the United States when we see stores full of food and we pay farmers not to grow? Who would not be confused as we see such problems here in America, knowing we are sending our food and our dollars overseas? Did you know that there are statistics that show one in four children in America is going to bed hungry? For this reason it is easy to see why so many logical thinking people actually believe "they (the government) can do something, but they don't want to"?

Now, let's just follow that logic. Who is this "they"? The mayor of what city, the governor of what state, what president would not eradicate poverty if he could? After all would eliminating poverty not guarantee his place in history as our greatest president ever?

Don't you believe that is what they really want? I am convinced that they would if they could and you should be too! However, like you they are blinded by the light and have succumbed to the teaching and lies that are not based in logic, reason or common sense or for the benefit of all the people, but that benefit only the 1%.

Since they cannot or will not do it, it is up to "We The People" to decide as to whether or not our children will be fed! If it is not their choice, it must become our choice to end poverty in the Unites States. It must become our choice to end the plight of the homeless, reduce crime, end inflation, lower or eliminate taxes, provide money for the cure of cancer, aids and all disease, and all the other things wrong with the world today. There is also this other thing. It all boils down to this! Either you vote for new economic laws to follow, or it is you and not them who can do something about it, but doesn't want to!

Do you really believe that all politicians past and present belong to a secret organization, where after meeting in some smoke filled room, they are told how the country's problems can be solved, but then they all swear never to reveal it! No the problem is this, they are kept blind to the simple solution before them by bankers, who don't want to bake a cherry pie, who don't like cherry pie and who are more than content with their lemon pie.

The problem appears to be this. For some reason (money and power), our Congress insist upon baking lemon pies, they insist upon using the same old ineffective policies of the past even though they know they didn't work thousands of years ago, hundreds of years ago, and they didn't work yesterday and they don't work today. Nor is there any reason to believe that they will miraculously work in the future.

So what is the quickest and easiest way to solve a hunger problem? It is to create a way that allows people to eat. Some way that will allow them access to the food that's so abundant. The quickest and easiest way to end a homeless problem is to create a way that allows the people access to the homes already so abundant or able to be built. Almost everywhere I go, I see vacant buildings, apartments for rent, and houses for sale. There are construction workers out of work. We also have plumbers, electricians, and carpenters who are in need of work. We see how fast we can put up a building. We have what we need to eliminate poverty. Then why don't we? What is the reason why after hundreds of years we are still in the same mess?

The reason for this mess should now be abundantly clear. We need to change our economic formula from one that is dependent upon limited monetary distribution, and rule by the minority to one that makes use of an unlimited money supply and rule by the people. Armed with these new Optinomic laws of economics and Constitutional Democracy, finding solutions to the real problems we face both today and in the future will become much easier.

What do you think? Are the solutions to our present and future problems more likely and more quickly to come from someone experiencing that problem, or from someone who has not? By calling on the minds of all Americans the likelihood that someone will have a solution to any problem is increased. Somewhere in America there is a person who holds the key to a better voting system, while still another will discover the cure for AIDS. There are those among us with good ideas for reducing crime, and for better ways of reducing the debt. Somewhere among us is even the solution that could end war forever.

In this world of today with all of its communication technology, the most illiterate people today are more informed than the most literate of people in the past. For this reason we should not judge books by their cover, nor should we judge the capability of a person by his education or the position he holds. To find better solutions more quickly and more accurately, our recipe must always avail itself to the ideas of the people. Are there solutions to our problems? I honestly believe so and I bet you do too! At some time all of us have had ideas on how things could be done differently . . . but what if you do have a good idea, new idea, or "A Better Way? Where do you go with it? Who is ready to listen to you? Who will give your idea a try? Can you give me the name of one governmental agency or official ready, willing and able to help or even listen to your idea?

Is it right to expect that just because we elect some people to office, our job is now done? Is it right to sit back and wait for them alone to find solutions? We have been waiting for quite awhile. Maybe it's time for a change? We are a government of the people are we not? Then why do we not act like one? Imagine an end to hunger and homeless, a reduction in crime, money for the research and the cure of all disease, FREE health care, FREE education and no more wars. In America whether we opt for change or to keep things as they are, is our choice.

THE NEW WORLD ORDER

The New World Order is coming; the evidence is all around us. The real question for concern is not when it will occur, but how will it occur? Will it be by the lies and decline of the Constitution from an oligarchy of non representing representatives, who themselves are ruled by an oligarchy of bankers and corporate CEO's, or are we going to bring forth an Optinomic American Evolution of, by and truly for the people.

Will we keep sending our sons and daughters to foreign shores to be maimed or killed, continue to see children both here and abroad dying of starvation and continue to allow our loved ones to suffer and die because of unaffordable healthcare or will we use our logic, reason and common sense to stop these things from happening? Let me ask you this? How many of us wish to see never ending inflation, the proliferation of crime and the use of recreational drugs to the detriment of its user continue?

For things to change we must act and we must act quickly to insure those blessings and liberties that we cherish most do not perish. So the question to you is this. Are you going to continue to elect representatives who continually refuse to represent? Who show no allegiance to you and who will say and do anything to get elected? Do you remember "Read My Lips" No New Taxes only to be followed by new taxes? Do you remember "The American People Will Have A Chance To Review A Bill Before It Goes To Legislation" and an end to the Patriot Act? The Patriot Act was renewed for 4 more years and how many bills have you had the opportunity to review?

Who among us is happy with the breakdown of the family and the absence of a parent being home to care for their children because both parents need to work just to merely survive? I am also quite confident that we also do not wish to see our present day freedoms and liberties taken away from us in the name of homeland security.

There is a concerted effort by an oligarchy of people who believe that they and not the people have an unalienable right to determine the course of human events. Their best weapon is ignorance, fear and control of the money. By instituting among us a fear that big brother is coming, they are able to create themselves as our big brother. Rather than us being afraid of big brother it is of the utmost importance for us to create a new world order where big brother is afraid of us.

Let's review some policies we follow today. Are these policies positive (OPTINOMIC) or negative (Pessinomic) influences in our lives? Should they continue or is there a need for change? It's your choice.

First: Should we continue to allow hunger and homeless, or poverty in general to exist, or is there need for change?

Second: Has the quality of life improved to the best it can be, given our technological advances, or is there need for change?

Third: Is the political process truthful, and the best it can be, or is there need for change?

Fourth: Do we continue to use a method of taxation that burdens wealth and perpetuates inflation, or is there need for change?

Fifth: Do we continue to follow economic policies that allow some to have more only by causing others to have less or even not at all, or is there need for change?

Sixth: Is your present and future as financially secure as you would like it to be, or is there need for change?

Seventh: Have the Health-Care and Educational systems in this country improved or declined? Are they affordable and equally available to all, or is there need for change?

Eighth: Do we continue to be subjected to the illegal Federal Reserve and 16th Amendment, or is there a need to change?

Ninth: And last but certainly not the least, do we continue to be ruled by the minority as a Republic unable to truly voice our opinion on all the issues that affect us, or is there a need to change?

We can either use our technology to finish the job that our forefathers have begun, and make the changes we need and desire, or we can continue to see our Constitution and our freedoms to erode and be violated. While instituting Optinomics in a Republic such as ours would be a good thing, it is my belief that only in a Constitutional Democracy could Optinomic principles flourish to the best they can be.

Armed with our new knowledge we no longer need to feel hopeless or helpless. If you agree that there is a need for change, then you must realize that actions speak louder than words. You must also understand that in unity there is strength, united we can succeed and divided we will fail. You must act in order for things to change. To change or not to change, to vote or not to vote, is there really a choice?

Since it is abundantly clear that for us to keep using a limited money supply to create and distribute the wealth of this nation should change, is there something we can use that could easily replace it? Yes there is. It is also something very familiar to us and we have been successfully using it for a long time. It is called a credit or debit card. Credit cards use numbers and numbers are unlimited. What is the last number?

Here's something else to think about. It is also something that I believe should ease our fears about possibly losing our money on deposit in a bank. If your money in the form of credits is already in your account and guaranteed by the federal government, how could there ever be any runs on the bank?

If a bank were to fail, it would simply because of their inability to make a profit. This would also be most likely due to competition or poor management. In that case in a FREE market society that bank should fail. However, since all credits are insured by the government and could be immediately replaced, you could never lose your credits. So upon their failure your credits (money) would just be transferred to another bank. The other good thing about numbers is that numbers are not only positive, but numbers can also be negative.

The fact that an account can go negative is very important. It is the use of negative numbers that will finally allow some to have or have more without causing another to have less or none at all.

If our two main economic concerns are the laws of supply and demand, is it not then reasonable to conclude that an individual has a certain inherent credit and worth? Democracy says it does.

After all, is it not the individual who is at both the supply side and at the demand side of the equation? For this reason it is of primary importance that all the people be kept healthy, fed, clothed, housed, and educated. It is also very important that they are FREE to go wherever they may need to go to produce those goods and services. It is also of equal importance that they be FREE and able to express their ideas.

Because economic laws are not God given and that "We The People" may opt to make the economic laws by which we shall abide, and because the use of a system of debits and credits appears to be the new best way for now to do this, what we must next decide is how do we debit and credit these accounts. There seems to me to be seven main ingredients that are necessary to bake that cherry pie of prosperity. Seven ingredients that must be made available to all the people all of the time! If you can think of more please email to ingredients@cvaol.com

THE AMERICAN WEALTH CARD!

The First ingredient at the top of this list is Health-Care. If an individual is not healthy will they be more or less productive? The answer to this question makes it obvious that health-care should be universally available and affordable to all. Don't you agree?

The Second ingredient is Education. Should a person know how to do their job in the best manner possible? You bet. Since education by its very nature always improves society and promotes the general welfare, it too must be universally available and affordable to all. Right?

The Third ingredient is Food, The Fourth ingredient is Clothing, and The Fifth ingredient is Shelter. If we go without either of these for any extended period of time, it is unlikely anyone will stay healthy.

The Sixth ingredient is Transportation, and The Seventh ingredient is Communication. Both transportation and communication are vitally important for the production of goods and services.

These are the seven main ingredients for the making of that cherry pie of prosperity. However the ingredients alone are not enough, we must also have the proper recipe too.

Practical Application. So then how do we create these seven main ingredients, so we can bake that cherry pie of prosperity? It is as simple as Congress passing the proper legislation. Legislation that makes our present social security cards, the new American Personal Wealth Card and declaring the credits contained therein to be legal tender for all debts public and private. The Social Security Administration could also be put in charge with dispersing the new credit card and insuring that every citizen receives one.

Below is a chart that outlines what I believe to be the main problems facing Americans today. In the next two columns, I have listed our present solutions and the results of Optinomics solutions.

PROBLEMS AND INJUSTICES	Present Solution	Optinomic Solution
Ping-Ponging of Wealth	None	Ended
Hunger and Homeless	None	Ended
Inadequate Clothing	None	Ended

Unfair Taxation	None	Ended
Runaway Inflation	None	Ended
Children Being Left Alone	None	Ended
Declining Standard of Living	None	Ended
Problems with Immigration	None	Ended
Employment	None	Assured
Health Care and Education	None	Assured
Social Security Benefits	None	Assured
Research Money for Disease	None	Assured
Money for Self Defense	None	Assured
Money for Desired Programs	None	Assured

We can also charge our present social security department with the duty of administering these new benefits. Through the use of the American Personal Wealth Card everyone American would be guaranteed COST-FREE health-care and COST-FREE education. Through the use of the Personal Wealth Card all who need to eat will be fed. All who are in need of clothing will receive it. All who need to get to work will have a way to do so. Every American's social security shall be guaranteed. This will create a stronger economy and a higher standard of living for all of us, and for all future generations.

My proposal for The American Personal Wealth Card's features and benefits are listed below. I believe them to be a good starting place to be opened for debate. I also believe however, it ultimately should be left to the people to vote upon what they should be.

Hunger Feature: Any approved business accepting the American Wealth Card for the purpose of the sale of food or groceries shall be duly credited and, the buyer's account shall be debited.

Positive Results: Since an account can go negative anyone who is hungry can eat, even if they lack the credits in their account. The benefit to the business will be a credit in their account thereby allowing them to cover their costs and make a profit too.

Clothing Feature: Any approved business accepting the American Wealth Card for the purpose of the sale of clothing shall be duly credited and, the buyer's account shall be debited.

Positive Results: Since an account can go negative anyone in need of clothing may receive clothing. The benefit to the business will be a credit in their account thereby allowing them to not only cover their costs, but to also make a profit too.

Housing Feature: Any approved account accepting the American Wealth Card for the purpose of the payment of rent or for a residential mortgage. That account shall be duly credited and the user's account shall be debited.

Positive Results: Since an account can go negative, this will insure housing for all. The benefit to all landlords will be a guarantee of their rent to make needed repairs and insure against foreclosures.

Communication and Transportation Features: Any approved business accepting the American Wealth Card for the provision of transportation and or communication shall be duly credited and the buyer's account shall be debited.

Positive Results: Since an account can go negative, the person in need of transportation to get medical care or to report for work will be able to do so. The benefit to the businessman is a credit in their account. This credit will cover their costs, and insure them a profit.

Education and Health-Care Features: Any business accepting the American Wealth Card for the purpose of providing health-care or education shall be duly credited and, the buyer's account shall NOT be debited.

Education and Health-Care should be treated a little differently because of their importance to society. A person's health is imperative to the production of not only the supply side of economics but also to the demand side as well. Therefore the health of an individual is equal to any expense it may occur. For this reason no additional debit to their account should be made. The same applies to education. A person's education is their credit to society and so no additional debit to their account should be made.

Positive Results: If you can now go to any doctor you desire. What do you think will happen to the medical profession? Since hospitals and doctors will be able to charge whatever a Free Market economy will bear, money will not prevent them from doing a good job. If they do this good job the people will go to them. If they don't they won't. This will attract more and better hospital and doctors and should also eliminate those long waits we all hate.

The same applies to education. Because everyone can now afford an education, schools can charge whatever a FREE Market will allow to attract the best teachers and to build the best facilities. Since a student can now afford to go to any school he or she desires. A school will have to be the best it can for it to be chosen. This will produce the competition we desire without any limitations. Because of this a student will need better grades to get into the better school, however a lack of funds will no longer prevent anyone from getting a top-notch education or receiving terrific medical care.

Negative Account Remedies: We should not forget that the main goals of our economic policies must be to address the laws of supply and demand. We must also keep in mind that this means the people must be motivated to be productive. With this in mind I propose that a negative account should be restricted as to what merchants will be approved. For example with regards to hunger I would propose a fast food chain may be granted the right to allow an account to go negative but a fine steak house would not be able to do so. For the buying of clothing perhaps thrift store would be the way to go and so on. We should provide for adequate needs while creating motivation and desire.

Crime: How much crime is committed because of the necessity to eat, to pay one's rent, and to clothe oneself and their families? How much crime would be prevented if all transactions in a person's account were traceable and transparent? How would one buy stolen property, offer or accept a bribe, or buy and sell illegal drugs if one had to show from where they were debited and to whom they were credited? How many people would commit a crime, if they knew they would have to account for these debits and credits in their account? How much better off would we be If every parent had their child's credit card statement come to them for review?

Motivation and Punitive Relief: Since it is of vital importance that we motivate the people to be productive, any purchase we allow to go negative in an account should be very limited. Thus the person desiring a car is kept motivated to be productive. Also as part of the law, the people should be allowed to vote for punitive relief to discourage any abuse of the law. For this reason we should also limit the amount of time any account may remain negative.

Ninety days seems to be a reasonable amount of time for someone to straighten out his or her finances. However, if someone was unable to do so in whatever the period of time the voters determined it should be. After that time, any account that remains negative should be subject to review. The holder of such a negative account shall be made to appear before a regulatory agency. My thoughts are we should give our present social security administration the authority to handle this task or perhaps the IRS. The person being summoned will have the opportunity to explain why their account is negative. If a person lost a job, or has some other problem or legitimate excuse for their account being negative, the agency assigned to this task should have the authority to do whatever it takes to remedy the situation. Given the problems and solutions listed above. A person would be foolish NOT to vote for a change. The choice is ours. Which is "A Better Way"? Which will you choose? Also keep in mind if it is the people who are making the laws, then it is not Big Brother watching us, but we who are watching Big Brother. That's what government of, by and for the people means.

Can you imagine you or a loved one being sick and all you needed to do was call your physician for an appointment and after being seen on time, you simply handed the receptionist your American Wealth Card, signed for services rendered, and walked out the door? Can you imagine needing a prescription filled without the fear of what it will cost? Can you imagine, God forbid, being hospitalized or needing surgery, without having the added stress of becoming bankrupt because you were not covered by insurance, or your insurance company refused to approve payment?

Can you imagine sending your children to whatever school you desired and upon registration all you needed to do was to hand the bursar your American Wealth Card and all the classes, lab fees, books, trips, sport fees and whatever else concerning your child or your own education for that matter were paid?

Can you imagine losing your job without the stress and fear of losing your apartment or home, because of an inability to make the rent or mortgage payment, or being unable to feed or clothe your loved ones?

Can you imagine what it would be like to know that you would quickly be able to find another job that made use of your skill, education and likes because of the American Job Assurance program?

Can you imagine no poverty, less crime, and an overall higher standard of living and honest representing representatives? Imagine being able to achieve all the things we can't today simply because of a lack of money. How would you like to live in that kind of an America? Well you can, all you need to do is choose to make it so.

WE THE PEOPLE!

We the people, in order to form a more perfect union, provide for the common defense, promote the general welfare, and ensure the blessings of liberty, to our ourselves, and our prosperity do hereby ordain and establish this Coalition of Voting Americans. Can we form a more perfect union without actually doing it? Of course not, but what if we could create a coalition of the people, by the people, and truly for the people?

With the help of the Internet could you imagine what such a communicative network could achieve? Whatever your personal feelings regarding unions, there are some undeniable facts. They are: UNITED WE STAND, DIVIDED WE DON'T JUST FALL WE FAIL AND IN UNITY THERE IS STRENGTH.

A single opinion is seldom heard, but put enough opinions together, and you can make the law. After all, what is the law? The law is the will of the people. It is the mandate of the majority, or is it? Do the majority of the people want the POVERTY so prevalent in the U.S. today? I don't think so! I also find it hard to believe THE HUNGER, THE CRIME, THE DRUG ABUSE, and THE HOMELESS PROBLEM here in America today is the will of the people. Is it your will? It is if you do noting to stop it. How can we promote the general welfare, if we don't unite to do so? How do we ensure the blessings of liberty to our prosperity and ourselves without changing the power of our so-called representatives?

Representatives who with just one vote, which never is ours, can increase our taxes. Representatives who with just one vote, which never is ours can involve us in a war. Representatives who with just one vote can institute policies of non-productivity! Representatives who with just one vote have the power to build unlimited numbers of weapons of mass destruction! We must find a way to prevent their one vote from superseding the will of the people. They should also be denied the power to institute and perpetuate policies that create inflation. Policies that make the average citizen unable to provide for themselves and their family. To achieve this we must re-create the Democracy our founding fathers envisioned and we must re-create it now. Only through true Democracy could we ever hope to be truly represented!

Just like Dorothy in the Wizard of OZ, Americans have always had a way home. It is called the power of the vote. Voting for change is as easy as was going home for Dorothy by clicking her heels. It is as simple as doing it. What we need today is our network. A network of, by and for the people that will seek out and find solutions to the problems we face. A network of people that worked together not against each other. Excepting perhaps, David slaying Goliath, no great evil has ever been overcome without the people being united.

We know that corporations are united and have their lobbyists to achieve what they want. Labor is united to achieve what it wants. Political parties are united to elect politicians who take our votes and our money. Politicians who then normally do just the opposite of what they promised to do. Sure I'll vote. I'll vote when that vote really makes a difference. Isn't this the feeling of most Americans?

We don't need to provide unemployment insurance, what we need to provide is employment assurance. We need a network that will guarantee to promote the general welfare by making known the social, economic, and political injustices of the day. Do you believe like me that America is more than just a place, that it is also a state of mind, and that to be an American means to be free? Free to have your ideas heard and to express your viewpoint without fear of ridicule. Free to judge social reform programs before, not after they become the law. If you do! Then you must give up that label that divides us and help us change what we all agree needs to be changed.

So here is the plan in a nutshell. Before we can bring about the economic, social, and political reform that we desire. We must first bring about a communications network, a coalition of voters to state just what our needs, wants, desires, and fears actually are. Could you support a network that actively worked toward finding real solutions to real problems? What if this network could make the dream of the American Personal Wealth Card come true? Could you add your voice to ours then? Imagine what we could accomplish if we were free of the political mechanism of red tape and waste. Now imagine an America united together, a truly Democratic America united toward a common goal. Bobby Kennedy said it best when he paraphrased George Bernard Shaw and said, "Some see things that are and ask why. I dream of things that never were and ask why not?

THE CVA AND THE VOTERY

To implement the principles of Democracy and Optinomics and to bring forth the ideas of the people and their solutions to the ills of the day, I submit for your approval the CVA. This Coalition of Voting Americans will sponsor a series of forums on the Internet and wherever else possible. These CVA forums shall be called "The Votery" and will motivate people to participate through a lottery-like reward.

The CVA shall engage the participation and support of all the people, governments and corporations. However it is our intent to proceed with "The Votery" should such participation or cooperation by the governments fail! Using a format similar to America's Got Talent The CVA will be producing "America's Got Ideas" which will allow the people to make known their solutions to various problems in different categories such as healthcare, education, political reform, banking reform and others.

Till we can produce a live TV show we will be using the Internet to allow the people to upload their solution to be voted upon by a panel of judges and the people. To help with the deciding of the categories, and problems to be solved, the CVA requests that the people at large make their thoughts known on what they should be by visiting http://cvaol.com and suggesting desired categories and problems to be solved and by voting on those already presented.

The CVA intends to offer a monetary reward based upon participation by both contestants and voters through advertising and lottery like dollars received from those voting. To be an eligible contestant all one needs to do is to submit their ideas and solutions in a text or video outlining his or her solution to one of the questions posed, and then upload it to http://cvaol.com so that it may be viewed and scrutinized by potential voters. The winning contestants, like on "America's Got Talent", and in the true spirit of Democracy will be determined by a vote of the people.

The funds raised by the Votery shall be distributed in the following manner. 10% of the funds raised by the Votery shall go into the CVA treasury for administrative costs and advertising. 10% of the funds raised by the Votery shall go to implement the program of the people's choice. 10% of the funds raised by the Votery shall go into the next level up contest to increase its treasury. The CVA goal is to sponsor not less than one contest in each Zip Code, Area Code, State, Time Zone and Nationally. 10% of the funds raised shall go to motivate participation in "The Votery" by rewarding the winning contestant with a cash prize. The remaining 60% of the funds raised by the Votery shall go to motivate the average citizen to participate by the chance of a cash reward for their participation through their vote.

The CVA holds the Votery is a logical use for America's lottery fever, as it will offer solutions to the very real problems facing us today. The CVA foresees an army of contestants consisting of "Domestic Warriors" and "Planet Patriots" who will offer their solutions in our battle against the forces of ignorance and poverty.

As we have seen through various wars, a coalition of different interests is an effective way to achieve victory. So our first attempt will be to form a coalition of our present political parties, organizations and corporations. However, if we cannot get our present political leaders to put their differences aside so that America can come first, the CVA will then seek out and find candidates of its own behind who this country can rally. The CVA endorsed Candidate will truly represent the will of people, because to receive our endorsement a candidate must pledge and sign a legal and binding contract. This contract states that if they do not vote the wishes of the people, they will resign from office. The CVA endorsed candidate shall be elected by the people with the full knowledge that they will work toward the repeal of the income tax amendment and to abolish or dramatically change the Federal Reserve. The contract also states that they pledge to foster and create new policy based upon the principles of Optinomics and unlimited monetary supply economics.

In addition and as part of the contract, each CVA representative agrees to also conduct town hall meetings to discuss the legislation before them with the people who elected them. It also states that the CVA endorsed candidate will vote not their wishes or the wishes of their party, but they will vote on the legislation before them in Congress as per the wishes of the majority of their constituents. The job of the CVA representative shall not be to explain their personal feeling on any matter, it is to explain ALL sides to any proposed legislation the best they can so that the people may decide which is best for them.

Those candidates receiving CVA endorsement must also pledge themselves to support "The Votery" so that we may draw upon the minds of all Americans and not just those few belonging to some political party. To find the solutions we seek, their allegiance must be to the American people. It must also be to foster Optinomic principles, the Personal Wealth Card, to end the laws of limited supply, and to finish the reason for the birth of this nation and the intent of its founding fathers.

When given a choice between a CVA endorsed candidate and a candidate who will not sign this contract, I believe such a choice will motivate the present eligible voters who do not vote to vote. What do you believe?

CHANGING THE WORLD
ONE VOTE AT A TIME

It is up to us to elect a new Congress. A Congress not of Liberals, Conservatives, Democrats or Republicans, but of Americans. With your vote that new Congress will not pass legislation and then present it to us as the law. Instead that new Congress will present proposed legislation for our approval before it is passed and made into law. Only then will the silent majority of Americans, no longer be silent. Who now cannot and must not be silent if we are to see the change that we so need and want.

Our political process as it stands today can never represent the wishes of the majority of Americans. If the majority of people are not ruling this country, then there can be no Democracy. If we truly desire to see this nation achieve its full potential. It must first be allowed to achieve and practice Democracy. However if we cannot, we should at least return to the representative Democracy as practiced in early America.

Now is not the time for us to continue to limit causing some to be left out. Now is not the time to continue to follow the failure proven Pessinomic policies of the past. Now is not the time to follow political leaders and parties that divide us rather than unite us.

Now is the time to institute a new economic and political formula that can work for all! Now is the time for us to give up the labels that divide us. Now is the time to recognize that there is only one race of people that counts. That race is not the white race, black race, yellow or red race. The only race that counts is the one that holds all those colors . . . the human race.

Now is the time for the people to take back this country and restore the democratic principles for which it stands. Now is the time to join together, to register and to vote. Now is the time to stop never ending inflation and to REPEAL THE INCOME TAX AMENDMENT! Now is the time to use the CVA advantage.

Now is also the time to call upon all Americans for their ideas on how to improve this nation's future. This recognition of the fundamental dignity and worth of the individual is as an important a principle of Democracy as is majority rule. The CVA lead will also foster and create new ways of economic and political cooperation. It will also lead the way in promoting caring and sharing and eliminating apathy and greed.

TO DREAM THE IMPOSSIBLE DREAM

At first, all this may sound impossible, but then again so did going to the moon, the horseless carriage (automobile), TV, electricity, and the best one of all, the Polio vaccine. Right Dr. Salk, you're going to prevent Polio by injecting people with the disease! No thanks! Would have been the response by most of the people. What would yours have been? What about today? Isn't it amazing how our perceptions change.

There is one thing that is certain. We will never effectively change the future for the better by continuing to do what has not worked in the past. Who hasn't had a difficult problem or task made easier once the proper tool was used or the "right" solution was known? Have you ever heard the expression "as plain as the nose on your face" or KISS "keep it simple stupid"? These simple but true expressions seem to be something today's politicians have forgotten.

Did you know that when the game of basketball first began, the basket had a bottom on it? For eight years, whenever a point was scored, the ball had to be removed from the basket. It's pretty hard to believe that it took eight long years before someone thought of simply letting the ball to fall through the basket. Can you imagine!

Is this really an impossible dream?

Today we had no homeless. Today all the people were fed.

Were the front-page headlines on the newspaper that I read!

Questions were asked. Starting with why wage we war?

For peace it was answered, but when pondered, all became sure

That killing and fighting and causing destruction

To peace is nothing more than obstruction.

Brother helped brother without regard to race, color, or creed.

Nor was there a mention of that word we call greed.

I remember a smile on my face. Why? Can you guess?

You would smile too if you were taxed less.

I recall a game show, "The Votery" and "A Better Way"

And Democracy, people voting, and having their say.

At last real solutions to real problems or so it did seem.

Committed am I, never to wake up from this dream.

If you can put the above to music, I would be very grateful.

Is this an impossible dream? What is impossible to dream is that we allow the nightmare of poverty, starvation, homeless, and disease to continue. More Americans have died from these ills of society than in all of our wars. What is impossible to dream is the way we have allowed the family to break down, allowed our children to not be taught right from wrong. We have removed parental guidance from the home.

Why is there no parent in the home to guide our children? Both parents are out working, not to live, but to merely survive. Does it really seem to anyone that this is the way it is supposed to be? There must be "A Better Way". Is this dream impossible, or is it a dream that can come true? It is up to WE THE PEOPLE to us to choose.

Do we continue to try to create a cherry pie using the lemons of limited currency and taxation, or do we develop new economics to coincide with the technology of today? Should we continue to climb the ladder of success, a ladder whose crossbars are so old and rotted that they break with each step we take, or do we reach beyond our wildest dreams and move upward with the simple press of a button that opens the doors of an elevator?

"I have a dream" (Martin Luther King). "Ask not what your country can do for you, ask what you can do for your country" (John F Kennedy). What can you do for your country? You can join and support the CVA, Democracy, Optinomics, the American Personal Wealth card and help in the birth of "A Better Way" and The American Evolution.

You can help us win the domestic war by actively participating in the Coalition of Voting Americans and by directing traffic to the CVA website http:// cvaol.com, and getting others to do the same. If you have a website you can help show your support by placing a banner on it. You can help through donations and buying this book and giving it away. You can help by submitting your name for an endorsement in your political run for Congress by signing the CVA candidates contract. You can help us create products to wear and display that will help spread the word. You can wear and or display a Red, White, and Blue "V" Ribbon, Flag or Sticker. "V" for Victory, "V" for the power of the Vote, Red, White and Blue for the real America, the America we hold in our hearts.

Your country needs you. It needs you to enlist into our Volunteer Army of Domestic Warriors. Our weapons are our ideas and our votes. Our command centers are Internet video and voice conference rooms with text capabilities. We use these rooms as headquarters for members to meet, exchange their ideas and to administer and foster the Votery and "A Better Way".

Please visit your local CVA headquarters often. If there is not a CVA divisional headquarters in your election district, please contact info@cvaol.com about how to create one.

WHAT'S IT REALLY ALL ABOUT?

What's it really all about? It's all about solutions to the problems of people and a representative government and a system of economics designed over 200 years ago. Are you really convinced that people who lived hundreds of years ago were somehow better able, than the people of today to develop a system of economics, government and banking for solutions to the problems of today? People who lacked all of the education, experience and technology of today? Even our founding fathers didn't think so, that's why they provided our Constitution with an ability to create Amendments as the needs of the people changed.

What's it really all about? It is also all about a system of banking created 400 years ago and the Federal Reserve created 100 years ago. With regards to our banking system it is all about economic solutions not designed by the people, nor by their representatives, but by bankers. Since it was a group of bankers who developed this system to facilitate trade and a median of exchange, to whose benefit does your logic, reason and common sense tell you they developed this system? Did they develop it out of the goodness of their heart for all the people? I don't think so, do you? Of course not, they developed it for their own gain. If not why did the top bankers of the day meet in secret to write the Federal Reserve Act and then sneak it through when most Congressman were away on Christmas leave? Did you know that is how the Federal Reserve came to be?

To learn more about money, banking, and The Federal Reserve, "No More National Debt" by Bill Still makes for perfect reading, as does "The Creature From Jekyll Island" by G. Edward Griffin. You will also find innumerous other resources at http://cvaol.com. Only by educating the American voter can we ever hope to change the things that need to be changed. It is said that the devil has no better weapon than to cause you to believe he doesn't exist.

What's it really all about? It's all about people not going hungry and living on the streets and in poverty, so that others may live in lavish luxury. What's it really all about? It's about children not being properly educated, not because we don't have the technology and tools today to educate them better than ever before, but because we can't due to a lack of money that we can create! What's it really all about? It's all about whether we have respect for the elderly and refuse to allow them to choose between their medications and food! What's it really all about? It's all about sending our loved ones to fight in wars abroad to make the supreme sacrifice believing false pretense and lies.

What's it really all about? It's all about the Constitution and American freedoms being slowly and systematically being taken away! What's it really all about? It's all about a representative government and representatives who will not, cannot and refuse to represent the people. What's it really all about? It's all about a system of economics that only allows some to have or have more by causing others to have less or not at all! What's it really all about? It's all about conquering us by dividing us into states of blue and red instead of uniting us into states of red, white and blue. What's it all about? It's all about whether or not we are going to do something about it, or are we going to continue on blind faith and forego using our logic, reason, and common sense?

Make no doubt about it; there is no greater threat to our security and way of life than ignorance and tolerance. What's it really all about? It's all about you! Will you keep your label that divides us even though it hasn't mattered who's in charge, or will we come together as one voice and vote for change, real change. A change from doing what's right for some to doing what's right for all. What's it really all about? It's about whether we stay the Divided States of America or once again become the United States of America? What's it all about? It's about whether or not we will ever be a government that is truly of the people, by the people and for the people!

WHEN IS ENOUGH . . . ENOUGH

When the weapons of mass destruction turned out not to be true, one would have expected that the American people would become up in arms about it, but they weren't. Then when it was announced that American government was torturing suspected not convicted terrorists, and using rendition a practice where we kidnap people and turn them over to regimes that specialize in torture, I was sure now the American people would scream out in protest, they remained silent.

Then came the news that our government arrested thousands of so called terrorists and sent them to prison without a fair trial, or any trial at all for that matter, in fact they were not even afforded the right to confront their accusers. Now we will see America's outrage spearheaded by thousands of college students marching in protest, but there wasn't. As if this was not enough, when it had been discovered that the Executive branch of our government has been spying for years on ordinary law abiding citizens like you and me, surely this I thought was going to be the straw that broke the camels back, but it didn't! Destroying basic civil liberties enumerated in the Constitution, including our Bill of Rights, torture, unauthorized search and seizures, illegal wire tapping, war on false pretense. None of these things seem to offend today's Americans.

Had this happened in the 60's there is no doubt in my mind that you would have see hundreds of rallies and protests, but today there are no organized protests, no rallies, no media exposing what is happening. Excepting the TV series Boston Legal that did an episode exposing all of this, I am told while, G.W. Bush was still in office, it's as if none of these rights no longer hold importance to the media or the American people.

As unbelievable as all of that may seem, we have even lost the right to free speech and no one seems to care. Did you know that if you are at a presidential rally and have on a supportive tee shirt you could stay? However, if you have a tee shirt with an opposing message, or are supporting an opposing view you can be removed. They call these Free speech zones, but speech here is not FREE. Instead it is designed to contain Free Speech. No Free speech in the United Sates of American, can you believe it? You better because it is true.

Of course those who have the courage to object to this dismantling of the Constitution and our Bill of Rights, these patriots are labeled Un-American. I may disagree with what you say, but I will defend to the death your right to say it, are the words of every true American! In recent years nine of the ten guarantees in the Bill of Rights have been removed from our civil liberties. The only one you don't have to worry about is quartering soldiers, but that can be removed with the stroke of a presidential pen. I know I am not the only one concerned about these things? I know I cannot be the only one aware of them? God help us if I am! When is enough, enough? When you say it is!

The battle plan is simple. First we must allow the truth to be known about our present day economic and political system by creating a CVA chapter in each election district to promote Optinomics and a Constitutional Democracy.

Next we must help CVA endorsed candidates capture the majority of seats in Congress and the Senate so that at long last we can make the real changes needed by this country. Finally we must use our CVA headquarters to get the people participating in the Votery and "A Better Way".

The American Evolution with the help of Optinomics, The CVA, America's Got Ideas and The Votery can pave the way to protect our precious freedoms and allow not just some of the people, but all of the people, a way to achieve The American Dream. Most important of all, The American Evolution will stop the insanity, end our nightmare, change what needs to be changed, and make my incredible dream come true? Will you join me and take the pledge?

THE MEMBERS PLEDGE

Be it known now and in the future, as a member of the Co-Voters of America that I pledge to do the following:

1. To foster and support the principles of Optinomics and a Constitutional Democracy.

2. To support the Votery, and "America's Got Ideas", a lottery-like reality show, where questions and answers are brought to the table by ordinary citizens.

3. To support the American Personal Wealth Card.

4. To attend online town meetings to hear and discus both sides of an issue and to offer my input and if I have them my ideas.

5. To vote on proposed legislation whenever possible recognizing the importance of my vote to the principles of democracy.

6. To support to the best of my ability and vote for CVA endorsed candidates.

7. To support making campaign promises binding and to hold elected official guilty of defrauding the people when they break a promise, and if they fail to resign to support a recall.

8. To remove myself from membership if I fail to do any of the above.

THE REPRESENTATIVES PLEDGE

Be it known now and in the future, that in return for the CVA support if I am elected. I pledge to do the following:

1. To foster and support the principles of Optinomics and a Constitutional Democracy.

2. To support the Votery, and "America's Got Ideas", a lottery-like reality show, where questions and answers are brought to the table by ordinary citizens.

3. To support the creation of the American Wealth Card.

4. To regularly hold online town meetings to discuss social and economic problems and their possible solutions.

5. To explain in online town meetings the pros and cons of proposed legislation and to vote as per the wishes of my constituents.

6. To support to the best of my ability and to vote for other CVA endorsed candidates.

7. To implement my promises and to support making campaign promises binding or be held guilty of defrauding the people.

8. To remove myself from office if I fail to do any of the above.

Please visit The Co-Voters of America on line website at http://cvaol.com and become a member, candidate or election district leader. Our future is up to you!

THE BEGINNING

It Takes Money To Make Things Happen

Until we do make the changes we so desperately need and want, it will take your financial support to get things going and to spread the word. Think about what is at stake!

- A universal and FREE Health Care Plan for All

- A universal and FREE Education for All

- An end to hunger, homeless and poverty in general

- Unlimited resource money for cancer, aids and all disease

- Taxes drastically reduced or eliminated

- Crime drastically reduced or eliminated

- No more government borrowing or national debt

- Employment assurance for all

- The government really run of, by and for the people and more

Please buy and give this book away and donate generously at http://cvaol.com

All profits will go to purchase this book to be given away in digital and print form, the advertising of The CVA and for the production of videos to further explain Optinomics, Constitutional Democracy and to help candidates who have taken the pledge to get elected.

This is Not
THE END

It is THE
BEGINNING

www.ingramcontent.com/pod-product-compliance
Lightning Source LLC
Chambersburg PA
CBHW052244290526
45785CB00016B/1287